FOR EVERYTHING A SEASON

FOR EVERYTHING A SEASON

Prayer-Poems of Our Time

by

MICHAEL WALKER

Published by

ARTHUR JAMES LIMITED

THE DRIFT, EVESHAM, WORCS.

First edition 1971

© Arthur James Limited 1971

All rights reserved by the Publishers,
Arthur James Limited of Evesham, Worcs., England

ISBN: 0 85305 182 8

BIBLE QUOTATIONS

From the Revised Standard Version of
the Bible, copyrighted 1946 and 1952.

MADE AND PRINTED IN GREAT BRITAIN BY PURNELL AND SONS, LTD.
PAULTON (SOMERSET) AND LONDON

DEDICATION

To
The Memory
of
My Mother

FOREWORD

by

Dr. Howard Williams, B.A., B.D.
Minister of Bloomsbury Central Baptist Church, London.

AN OLD FRIEND of mine in Yorkshire put into a short, sharp sentence the lingering belief in the Priesthood of all Believers. When the Minister called, at the point of death, he dismissed him with the words, "I can pray for 'missen'."

Yet a problem with prayer is that when people had claimed right of way to God they had no longer any desire to walk that way. There are books full of beautiful prayers and patient advice from centuries of priests but the open way is a long way and people suspect that it is a dead end.

Michael Walker begins where people are. In work and play, sickness and health, love and hate, life and death, height and depth, all these experiences are here in their joy and sorrow. He doesn't invite us to travel round the world in order to get to where we think we want to be. He shows us how we can begin just where we are. I believe he begins in the right place and by lifting the latch of the door of our imprisoned room he encourages us to look into eternity.

I think, too, that Michael Walker's understanding of moods and tensions helps him to be a better guide than most.

FOREWORD

He is not like a man shouting about the resurrection havin
no experience of death.

There are lovely things in this book but it is the strength
rather than the beauty, which holds. Much of the book re
minds me of the conversation in prayer which I often hear
as a boy where intimacy and awe mingled. The serious moo
prevails but there is also the common—and comical—touc
in understanding human lives. From desperate situations th
cry comes as in the negro prayer, "O Lord, help me to under
stand that you ain't going to let nothing come my way tha
you and me together can't handle."

1971   HOWARD WILLIAMS

8

PREFACE

A BRAVE MAN once affirmed that there is no place where God is absent. Make up a bed in hell, he said, and even 1ere you will find Him. We all have areas in our lives where eaven has a foothold. But for the rest it is full of trivialities, :petition, and a few tears. Too often the good parts of life re where we expect to find God and we do the best we can 'ith what remains.

I have taken the words of the Preacher in Ecclesiastes, not ecause I share his despair, but because I believe there is no scaping the "times" with which life faces us. We might wish fe could be healing without killing, peace without war, birth 'ithout death, dancing without mourning. But it can never e so. All that we can try to believe is that God is in all our times".

I realize that for some the problem is not finding it hard) believe that God is in our mourning, but getting even a limpse of Him in our dancing. Yes, He's in the dancing. .ike I said, I don't despair.

I have used only seven of the fourteen couplets in Ecclesi-stes because they were the seven on which my thoughts ave chiefly centred. They all have an "elemental" quality bout them.

I would like to thank the people who have helped in the

production of this book. First, my friend Walter Bottoms, th
Editor of the *Baptist Times* in whose columns some of thes
prayer-poems were first published; Margaret Grant an
many others for design and typing; the ever-helpful Ro
Russell of Arthur James Ltd., my publisher, for his enthusiasm
painstaking care and constant consideration; Howard William
for his kind Foreword and the inspiration I have derive
from his preaching; and, last of all, my wife who shared an
in some cases endured, the experiences out of which thes
prayer-poems were written.

MICHAEL WALKER

4 A Pleasant Enough Ward
5 The Time of Our Healing

CONTENTS

I

A TIME TO BE BORN AND A TIME TO DIE

II

A TIME TO PLANT AND A TIME TO PLUCK UP

III

A TIME TO KILL AND A TIME TO HEAL

IV

A TIME TO WEEP AND A TIME TO LAUGH

V

A TIME TO MOURN AND A TIME TO DANCE

VI

A TIME TO KEEP AND A TIME TO CAST AWAY

VII

A TIME FOR WAR AND A TIME FOR PEACE

For everything there is a season,
and a time for every matter under heaven:
    a time to be born, and a time to die;
    a time to plant, and a time to pluck up what is planted;
    a time to kill, and a time to heal . . .
    a time to weep, and a time to laugh;
    a time to mourn, and a time to dance . . .
    a time to keep, and a time to cast away . . .
    a time for war, and a time for peace.

The Book of Ecclesiastes III

I

A Time to be Born –
and a Time to Die

A LOVING CONCEPTION

Thou didst knit me together in my mother's womb . . . Psalm 139: 13

LORD, IT WAS the most momentous thing that ever happened
    to me, being born, I mean,
    yet I can't remember a thing about it,
    it has no place in my memory,
    it happened,
    and I am here.

I have to look at my own children to see what being born means:
    then I remember,
    remember the loving
        that gave the seed
            that made the child,
    and the months of carrying,
        the womb growing and expanding with the life inside
           it, the fears, the waiting, the comedy
           (she had a passion for kippers, of all things),
    and, at last, the birth day.

I remember seeing the woman I love
    holding the child that was the gift of our love,
    the girl I had married who was now the mother of my
        own flesh and blood,

an hour after travail—and already the pain
had slipped into the past.

I remember Dick holding our baby daughter,
standing there like a nonconformist Simeon,
holding her tiny hands to his near-blind eyes,
"Isn't it marvellous," he said,
"the detail, tiny fingers, all separate"
—and Kerr,
receiving and blessing her
in the name of Christ and the church.

Lord, we can't remember how life comes to us,
but we cling to it with passion,
we guard and protect our children
because, in spite of all the storms that may
one day gather about their heads,
we know that it is good to be alive,
we are grateful to have been born,
life has given us far more than it has taken away.

Lord, how wonderfully you have made us
that our loving and our conceiving should belong togethe
that in the ecstasy of our bodies,
the strange, joyful, loving, funny
union of a man and a woman—
you grant the gift of a new life.

I am grateful, Lord, for that time
when, in my unremembered past, I was born:
and I am grateful that I have shared in
the mystery of birth,
a mystery that began in the most dear and familiar thing

2

THE PLAY GROUP

Jesus said, "Let the children come to me, and do not hinder them; for to such belongs the kingdom of heaven." Matthew 19: 14

LORD, THEY'VE COME out for the sunshine today,
　　children, peeping from the shrubs,
　　　　singing at the top of the climbing frame,
　　　　talking about mum as the swings leap back and
　　　　forc.

There's Jillie in a bridesmaid's dress she sorted out of the
　　dressing-up box,
　　she wobbles along on a pair of silver high-heeled shoes,
　　clutching a sequined bag,
　　she always goes for the exotic stuff,
　　the Queen of Selwyn estate, at last recognised
　　　　and crowned.

Christine is cooking at the wooden stove where cotton-reels do
　　for controls,
　　she has thumped the willing dough into a pudding,
　　but dough pudding is so plain,
　　too plain for Christine,

21

helpers, wide-eyed at her skill, are sent to fetch
    leaves and grass,
and the mixing begins all over again.

Timothy, big smile in black Nigerian face,
    waves an old electric light switch,
        —at least, you think it's a light switch,
    he knows it's a camera,
    he runs to you, exploding happiness—
    "Smile," he shouts, holding the camera
    in front of you, "no, bigger smile,
    bigger, bigger"—then *click*,
        another photograph that will never be developed.

Sanjay is cooking as well,
    "What are you cooking there, Sanjay?"
    "Chicken curry and rice," he says
        —home from home!

Maureen peers at me through her spectacles,
    her mother is away in hospital,
    ask how she is,
    "She's coming home soon," says Maureen
        —Maureen hasn't sorted out the men
            from the women yet,
        they're all "Mrs".

There's a group round the wash-tub over there,
    more boys than girls,
    Trevor takes his washing-up seriously,
    endlessly splattering water out of a Squezy bottle,
    another fills a mug with water then empties it,
    fills it, empties it,

fills it, empties it,
but why the surprise?
had you forgotten the times you gazed at water
   —pounding seas, roaring water-fall,
   he holds them all in his small hands.

Let the little children come to me
   said our Lord:
   the walls of the Church surround these children
   in an embrace,
   Lord, may we surround them with the reality
   that is not contained within walls,
   the reality of that Kingdom
   of which they are the chief example.

3

ONLY SIXTEEN

Can a woman forget her sucking child . . .? Isaiah 49: 15

LORD, SHE WAS sixteen,
 doing well at school,
 she was generous and kind,
 then they met, and she loved him.

They were happy together,
 her friends said he was too demanding,
  but she was generous and kind and in love,
   she learned too late that he had
    demanded too much.

It might have been worse for her, Lord,
 her parents were hurt,
 they had their dreams that one
 day she would fall in love,
  that she would be married,
  surrounded by promises
  to love, honour, comfort and keep,
  and there would be children,
  born in love and security:
 but now, no matter how different from their dreams,
  they stood by her,

determined that she should carry her
child without anxiety,
and fulfil the sacred responsibility
of giving birth to the life
within her.

The boy stood by her too,
he promised he would do what he could,
but fatherhood he could not promise,
he could neither bear the child
nor take responsibility at its birth,
he had given life,
but to the child that was his
he could give neither shelter,
family, nor security.

She had to leave school, Lord,
she went away from home—even if her
parents tried to understand that didn't
mean the neighbours would,
and came a day she gave birth
to a son,
and came a day she became a
woman and a mother,
she was a child no longer.

She was kind, generous and loving,
and when they handed her child to her
love soared within her,
the ecstasy of a woman
holding flesh of her flesh
and bone of her bone,
life given and life received.

Yet Lord, it wasn't as it might have been:
a bouquet from her Mum and Dad,
six red roses from the boy,
> but no one else to share
> the joy and the sadness:
> one day, it might have been
> the most beautiful moment
> in her life,
>> one day,
>>> might have been,
>>> but not now.

She decided to have the baby adopted,
not because she wanted to be rid of him
> but because she believed he had the
> right to a father as well as a mother,
>> because he should have what she
>> had had, the security of the
>> family.

He went to a good home,
and so she tried to comfort herself,
but as long as she lived she would
never forget
> the day she turned her back
> on the child she had carried,
> given birth to, and nurtured:
> for she was generous and kind,
>> and her body cried for her,
> it was her nature to love,
>> and loving she gave away
>> the child she loved.

ord, two people were in love
and so many people bore the cost of their love;
be with her parents who believe
that they have failed;
be with the boy who began something
he couldn't finish;
be with the child and those who have
given him what life might have denied
him were they not there :

and Lord, be with her,
keep her generous and kind,
may forgiveness heal the wound
inside her,
and one day may she give
birth to another child,
that what might have been
may become
what is.

4

THE OLD FOLK'S HOME

My days are like an evening shadow . . . Psalm 102: 11

LORD, THROUGH THE windows the trees tell the passing of t
      days
  spring, summer, autumn, winter,
  another full year
  and the old is older
      —and how little the years mean:
      the first ten years of our lives are
        full of growth and change,
      the last ten are like the slow movement
        of the shadows on a summer's evening.

They sit here,
    always in the same seats,
      deaf ones who stare,
      others reading books with big print from the libra
      some, fingers bent from arthritis, knit,
      and the rest gaze at television—
      soap operas, quiz programmes, pop stars,
      the world is moving on
      though they stand still to watch it go by.

They're lucky here Lord,
> they each have a wardrobe and a dressing table,
> and the large dormitory is divided so that
>> there is some privacy when they go to bed,
>> there is space to keep clothes, a few photographs,
>> some books, a box of chocolates:
>> yes, they're lucky here, not like some of the others:
>>> the first day Mrs Lawrie went to the
>>> Old Folk's Home they emptied out her handbag
>>> to make sure there were no valuables in it—
>>> nobody had ever touched her handbag before;
>>> Carrie lay in a bedroom with nine others,
>>> one tatty bedside locker each, and a jam jar
>>> with flowers in it to share between them,
>>> a transistor crackled somewhere,
>>> but nobody was listening,
>>> they stared at each other,
>>> stared, and said nothing;
>>> they let Vi have her canary and kept it
>>> in the living-room,
>>> but she couldn't keep books by her bedside,
>>> and she loved books;
>>> Bill used to sit with his buttons undone,
>>> he was beyond pride and caring
>>> and nobody seemed to mind,
>>> clothes were something to shamble in and out of,
>>> morning and evening.

Lord, those who care for the aged do a job I couldn't do,
> give them the strength and kindness,
>> patience and cheerfulness
>> to do it;
> and may those who organize the care of the elderly,

government, local councils, hospital boards,
voluntary agencies, trustees—
may all of them create conditions in which
people can grow old with dignity,
enjoy the life that remains to them,
and die, cradled in love.

5

NOBODY LIVES FOREVER

Jesus said, "I am the resurrection and the life; he who believes in me though he die, yet shall he live." John 11: 25

LORD, I USED to think death was a long way away,
    something old people thought about,
    a morbid subject, strictly for the ghouls,
        —until Tim was killed.

We remember him, Lord,
    the way he used to race down the road,
    scooter gleaming with chrome,
    fur pelt waving from a bendy aerial,
        he was a good soccer player too,
        grew his hair like George Best,
        and ran circles around the defence;
    he used to play the guitar,
    he had us all learning those
        Sydney Carter songs,
        he was doing well at work,
        another two years and he would
        have finished his apprenticeship,
    and he and Penny had been going
            out together,
    they seemed to be in love.

31

We can hardly believe he's dead, Lord,
    we still expect him to walk in any
        moment,
    hear a scooter and you think it's him,
    we still sing the Sydney Carter songs
        and it's as if he's there,
    and we can't look at Penny's eyes,
        she looks sort of kicked,
        and we don't know what to say.

Lord, he had hardly begun,
    there were miles still to go,
        goals to be scored,
            things to be made,
                love to be offered,
                    songs to be sung,
    and none of them will be finished.

Lord, death is not a long way away,
    neither are You;
        there's another thing about Tim,
        we all remember the day he
            told us he had decided
            to be a Christian:
        he never went back on it;
    neither do You go back on Your word, Lord;
        sooner or later, we die,
        and You are the Resurrection
            and the Life.

6

PSALM TO THE LORD OF LIFE

e is the image of the invisible God, the first born of all creation . . .
Colossians 1: 15

LESS THE LORD whose name is Jesus,
    for He has come as a man and made holy our flesh,
    He has entered the darkness of our death,
        and look! on the third day He comes,
        bringing life in our death,
        opening the tomb to the new day,
        wiping the tears of those that mourn,
        opening the clenched hands of those who despair,
        breathing His breath into the hearts of men
            half-dead.

ess His name
    in the boundless skies
    where the moon drifts in grey silence
    and the sun roars with energy,
    the stars speed down the light-years,
    galaxy sings to galaxy,
    and the outer limits bend into God.

Bless His name
> in the mountains where the wind whispers
> and clouds shroud the rocks,
> where the eagle glides down the lonely sky
> and the furtive stag stands listening,
> where the stream dances over the stones
> and leaps in the tumult of the waterfall.

Bless His name
> in the cities of man
> where cars fly on the overpass
> and traffic lights blink coloured eyes,
> where the tower block juts its chin to the skies
> and footsteps clatter down the storied canyons.

Bless His name
> in our human life,
> may He be praised in the passion of our bodies
> and the tender touch of our flesh,
> hands laid in blessing, hands clasped in friendship,
> lips touched in love:
> in the tears that purge us and the laughter
> that restores us,
> in the troubling, aweful, splendid hope
>> of our youth,
> in the gifts and responsibilities
>> of our prime,
> in the contentment and benediction
>> of old age.

Bless the Lord, Jesus, the Christ
> all you, His little flock,
> whose arms embrace the world,

whose heart carries all the sorrows of men,
whose lips speak what God has done,
whose bodies stand erect in freedom
    and bowed in worship.

less the Lord of the third day,
    body, mind and soul of mine,
    for He has given life.

II

A Time to Plant —
and a Time to Pluck Up

I

THE FIRST PLANTING

And God saw everything that He had made, and behold, it was very good. Genesis 1: 31

LORD, THAT'S HOW it was in the beginning,
       finite matter, shaped with infinite artistry,
       made fair and glorious:
       and whatever we have done with the world
              You made,
              raping maiden nature,
              turning stewardship into tyranny,
       yet still it bears the mark of Your hand,
              a beauty that ravishes our eyes,
                     a sound that excites our ears
                     and sings in our blood,
                            a texture, sensuous and
                            full of delight.

Lord, You made beauty for the sake of beauty,
       needing no spectators to justify its existence,
       requiring no seeing eyes to bring it to birth:
              we do not see each of the thousand
              leaves upon a tree,

yet every one is traced with subtle
delicacy, like the practised doodlings
of a man with a lifetime to spare:
every second, countless waves break upon
countless shores,
and each a tower of water,
crowned with foam, gathering momentum,
cascading on rocks, powerful and exuberant,
a carnival in no need of an audience;

and as I hear the sounds of this city
in which I live,
I remember mountains not far away
where at this moment there is no sound
save the wind in the grass,
and a skylark hovering far above,
and a waterfall that thunders amongst the trees,
catching the sun's beams,
tossing them about like a demented
juggler,
and perhaps someone will walk in those
hills today, and see it all—
and perhaps there will be no one.

Lord, that is how You made the world,
· with a care that reaches into every
crevice of creation,
lavishing more beauty than our eyes
can contain.

When I look at Your creation, Lord,
it seems strange that I should ever doubt
Your concern for every individual human
being:

A TIME TO PLANT AND A TIME TO PLUCK UP

for what is a leaf,
    a wave,
    even a mountain,
    compared to a man?

2

WE'RE ONLY HUMAN ...

*Then the Lord God formed man of dust from the ground, and breathed
into his nostrils the breath of life: and man became a living being*
Genesis 2: 7

LORD, THERE IS something extravagant in the way You
    endowed man:
    You set him in the midst of beauty,
    and gave him the gift of creating beauty,
        from the first drawings on the walls of a cave,
        to Michelangelo's "David", da Vinci's "Madonna"
        and Picasso's terse figures;
    You surrounded him with sound,
    and gave him the gift of music,
        from the first note, blown through a reed,
        to Bach's fugues, Chopin's Etudes,
        and Brahms' symphonies;
    You set order in the universe, and gave him
    reason and intelligence,
        from the first word, to the brilliance of Socrates,
        the poetry of Hardy, the logic of Hume,
        the invention of Watt.

And all this is ours, because we are human,
    because You made us, Lord,

and breathed into us Your own breath:
yet it is by that same humanity
that we excuse ourselves,
acknowledging the fatal flaw
by which we all bear the name
of Adam,
the shadow that casts itself over
all our achievements;
the same energy that drives us
in love and kindness,
drives us in self-seeking and
cruelty:
the intelligence that enriches life
can also ingeniously pervert it:
and, beside all our beauty
is the ugliness that our busy hands
and empty minds have devised—
after all, Lord, we're only human.

Lord, teach us that this is not our excuse but
our judgment,
that because we are human, we are responsible,
and because we are responsible, we are answerable:
show us that whatever is corrupt and wicked
bears not the mark of our humanity,
but our inhumanity:
restore to us our lost humanity,
in that other Adam,
Who is light without darkness,
love that does not violate,
truth undimmed by error,
that other Adam,
the Son of Man.

3

THE WORKMAN

In the sweat of your face you shall eat bread . . . Genesis 3: 19

LORD, WAS THAT first Sabbath a festival of work?
the artist standing back from His creation,
surveying the mountains shaped in the
uprush of volcano and the grinding of glaciers,
running His eye through the spectrum of colours,
drinking in the beauty:

the workman celebrating His labour,
seas contained, rivers set in their courses,
earth fertilised, roots firmly planted,
the infinite variety of tree, flower,
fruit, vegetable:

the technologist rejoicing in His invention,
energy set in the world,
running through the earth,
locked in the atom,
driving all living things to survive,
to reproduce, to hunt, to build, and finally,
to think.

Lord, did You celebrate Your work on that
    first Sabbath day?
    did You glory in Your labour?
    when the morning stars sang for joy
        in a world that had been
            created,
                fashioned,
                    shaped,
                        constructed
    by that divine hand.

Lord, it is Your intention for us, that we should
    celebrate our work,
    thankful for the skills of eye, hand, mind and ear,
    that fill our days with challenge and reward,
    and contribute to the common life of the communities
    in which we live:
    grateful that we have been made men,
the creative children of a creating God,
    using pen, tool, instrument, machine,
    apparatus, to further the limits of
    creation:
    so You intend, Lord . . .

But it is not so for all of us,
    there is work that is without reward,
    filling the empty hours that remain
    outside the full hours of leisure;
    work that is monotonous,
        work that is degrading,
            work that asks nothing of a man.

Lord, we wait for the new creation,
    that came on that other Sabbath,
        the day of Christ's resurrection,
        when You fashioned life out of death:
        the new creation,
        in which all work is worship,
            our reasonable service.

4

THE HARVEST

While the earth remains, seedtime and harvest, cold and heat, summer and winter, day and night, shall not cease. Genesis 8: 22

LORD, THE EARTH has never ceased to bear food,
the annual ritual of death, birth, life
and decay is every year enacted,
the hard ground breaks,
the seed is sown,
the plant reaches for energy
in earth and sun,
the leaves sprout,
the blossom falls,
the fruit appears,
and the harvest
is gathered in.

Lord, there has always been the harvest,
but not always where it is most needed,
for Dives' table groans beneath his
food,
for him there is no harvest time,
no frugal season preceding wealth,
no lean years before the fat,

only continual plenty;
the foods may vary
but always there is enough;
he eats, casting anxious eyes to his diet sheet,
lest the harvest plenty clog his veins
and choke his heart
and destroy him;
for Dives, whatever the fortunes of flood and plague
the harvest always seems to be there;

but Lazarus still waits,
he now has dignity and
will not eat the scraps
    fed to dogs,
    for Lazarus is no beggar asking
    charity, but a free man demanding
    rights;
    yet he suffers,
        if earth is blighted, it is his earth,
            if floods come, they overwhelm
                him,
                he cannot always believe,
                like Dives, that nature is
                merciful.

Lord, all that hunger daunts us,
    it seems never to grow less,
        no matter what is done
            it is always two-thirds of the
            world's population that is hungry,
                it never becomes a half,
                always two-thirds.

ord, he haunts our days,
    hungry Lazarus at the gate,
    we cannot celebrate a harvest safely
    gathered in,
    only a harvest fairly shared.

III

A Time to Kill —
and a Time to Heal

VIOLENT: WHO ME?

*And when they were in the field, Cain rose up against his brother Abel,
and killed him.* Genesis 4: 8

LORD, WE DON'T LIKE to think we are violent people,
    we have no killer instinct
        —unless you count smashing a cricket ball
        in a thoroughly aggressive and un-English way,
        determined to win
        and clobber the opposing team,
        but that's not our fault and it's certainly not cricket,
        just a casualty of our modern pushing,
        violent way of life.

What's a cricket ball compared to the heads that get smashed
        —almost every day on the telly,
        broken heads,
        maimed limbs,
        inert bodies, lying in the road?
        God! other people are so violent.

But that's not us, Lord,
        we are gentle people,
        we wouldn't strike anyone
        and the thought of killing we abhor.

Nevertheless, excuse the Freudian slips in our conversation,
      Lord,
      You know—the things we say that aren't meant
      to be taken literally:
      "I could have crucified her"
      "If he comes near this house again I'll kill him"
      "These homosexuals want to be taken out and
         whipped"
      "If looks could kill . . ."
      "Sometimes I wish I had a machine-gun, I'd
         line the lot of them up against a wall . . ."
         —but, of course, it's just our way of speaking,
         though we've no objection to others doing
            the crucifying, the killing,
            the whipping, the beating and the hanging
            on our behalf.

We're deluding ourselves, aren't we, Lord?
      —it wasn't thugs and murderers who crucified You,
      it was virtuous men, protecting the things they
      believed to be right,
      standing by their principles,
      guarding their holy faith
      —it was men like us,
         worthy men who will not recognise that they
         are also violent and cruel men.

Lord, I can't escape my own violence and anger,
    but may I harness it to truth and justice,
    may my tongue not lash weaklings
    and be silent against tyrants,
    may I know when to fight for things
      I believe in,

when to turn over the tables
and shout for God,
may my aggression become the hard centre
of my love,
may I be bloody-minded in the cause of
    the oppressed, the rejected, and the forgotten,
may love be strong to create
and not leave strength to the hate that destroys.

LOVING ALL THE PEOPLE
ALL THE TIME

*Then he showed me . . . the tree of life . . . and the leaves of the tree
were for the healing of the nations.* Revelation 22: 1–2

LORD, WE SANG some missionary hymns in church yesterday,
    they were splendid, in an old-fashioned sort of way,
        all about the Good News being preached in
            other lands,
        and the Kingdom being set up on earth,
        and people of different nations walking
        hand in hand,
        and enemies being reconciled,
            captives set free,
            heathens seeing the light,
            darkness turning to dawning
              —the tunes were good as well, Lord,
                so we all got carried away.

But it was all as if we were singing about something
    thousands of miles away,
    about people we never set eyes on,
    and the Christians who were going to do all this
    preaching were the missionaries:
    and that is what made it unreal . . .

Lord, we are trying to work out brotherhood here:
 Mr and Mrs Bhala and their little boy
 live down the road,
 the nurses in our local hospital are Spanish,
 Italian, Chinese and Jamaican,
 a lot of our 'bus conductors come from Pakistan,
 there are dozens of Jamaicans in the factory
 down in the town:
 it's all happening here,
  the world has come to Walthamstow.
 But the brotherhood bit that we were singing
  about in church, seems to have got lost;
  some of our immigrants have been attacked
  at night,
  others have had to close down their shop,
  and even the Christians are saying we
  must be "realistic" and not expect people
  of different cultures to mix together.

Lord, those hymns are on trial,
 and the Gospel is on trial,
 for either we accept the neighbour we can see
 or stand judged by You, whom we cannot see,
 either Christ reconciles us here
 or there is no reconciliation in Africa,
 the Southern States, Eastern Europe,
 or anywhere else in the world.

Help us, Lord,
 to accept people of other races as they are,
 and not when they fit our cultural pattern,
 and help them, Lord,

to forgive the slavery to which we
brought their fathers,
and the poverty that came with
freedom.

Lord, the barriers are high,
and only Your Calvary love can break them
down,
for You alone can reconcile us to each other,
and both of us to God.

3

THE OUT-PATIENTS' DEPARTMENT

. . . they brought to Him all who were sick. Mark 1 : 32

ORD, LAST TIME I came I forgot my appointments card,
 I told the girl behind the desk that I could
   give her my name,
 but she said that wasn't much help,
 it was the number they needed:
 I wonder what his number is, over there
 (49986, broken ankle, one);
 we spend most of our time wondering—
   what's she here for?
   that's a nasty eye—wonder what happened?
   poor old dear in the wheel-chair,
    waiting for the ambulance, I suppose,
    been there an hour already.

There's not much else to do, Lord, except think and wait,
 I've had two cups of tea and a packet of
 'Nice' biscuits,
 I've read the paper,
 and the magazines here are the same as last time,
 a couple of copies of *Woman,* one fairly recent,
 April 1969—they're catching up!

and a copy of *Illustrated London News* for the toffs:
fancy Lady So-and-So getting engaged to him,
who would have thought it?

Some of the people are here for consultation,
some of them are a bit nervous, you can see it
from the way they walk off to the cubicle
when their name is called:
we want to know what's wrong, but we don't,
behind the curtains begins a journey that could
take us to the operating theatre and a few
weeks in hospital after that,
a mother worries about the children—who will look
after them whilst she's away?
a man worries about a job—there are redundancies
every week, will they hold the place open
for him?
and the aged worry—they feel too old to be
pulled about, and who'll come to visit them?

The nurses are kind, Lord,
they look younger than they used to;
they hold a nervous hand,
chat up a cantankerous old man who resents having
to be helped,
clean up a wound,
and find time for all the other demands of routine.

Lord, we are all still crowding around Your door,
sick people asking to be healed,
hoping that You will make our bodies better;
hoping too, that You will heal those other,
deeper wounds:

the fear,
the guilt that asks, "Why should this happen to me?"
the anxieties,
the sudden realisation that we are not as brave
    as we thought,
the waiting and uncertainty,
Lord, walk amongst us,
    let Your shadow fall across us,
    and heal us.

4

A PLEASANT ENOUGH WARD

Bless the Lord, O my soul . . . who heals all your diseases. Psa
103: 2, 3

LORD, IT'S A PLEASANT enough ward,
    they tell me it used to be a charity hospital
    and charity is cold;
    it must have looked bleak in the old days,
    but now there are these coloured curtains round
        the beds,
    and flowers all over the place—just like
        Uncle Bill's funeral (that's a daft thing
        to think about here!),
    and there are the nurses,
        the one from France who makes even a
        uniform look like something out of
        Christian Dior,
        and Miss Jamaica,
        all sunshine and jolly exhortation,
        and that freckly one from Somerset,
        plodding efficiency, for which I'm grateful—
        but have *You* ever seen her smile, Lord?

The operation seems to be all right, Lord,
    I'm glad they only kept me in bed for about
        a day,
    it's a bit degrading having to ask for everything
        you want,
    it was a struggle to get to the end of the ward,
        but it was worth it—
        I was a mobile, independent human being
        again:
    a bit different from poor old Jack over there,
        he's stuck in bed day after day,
        they even have to feed him.

They were late with the lunch today,
    a minute after time and still no sign of the trolley,
    silly how we fret, but the routine seems to take over,
        and a minute is no longer a triviality;
    I suppose the surgeon's round put them behind—
        do You know, that's more awesome than
        church, Lord:
        he comes in here like a high priest surrounded
        by bowing acolytes,
        and I just sweat until he reaches my
        bed;
            he studies my temperature chart as if
            it were a confession of sin,
            still, he's made me better,
            so who's worried about
            the bedside manner?

Here come the visitors, Lord,
    clutching bags of fruit like Moses' spies;
        "I've used up the orange squash.

Any letters for me?
How are the children?
Good crowd at church yesterday?
Yes, he says I'm doing very well—just
    another five or six days.
Hold my hand."

That's how it is, Lord;
    they are all looking after me so well,
    Your healing hands are everywhere.

5

THE TIME OF OUR HEALING

Those who are well have no need of a physician, but those who are sick;
I came not to call the righteous, but sinners. Mark 2: 17

LORD, THERE IS a time when I need Your healing:

the time of others' violence,
when words have bruised me
and rejection has stunned me,
when the hurt they have done me
has left anger and resentment
festering inside me,
when I have nursed my grievance
like a serpent at my breast;

the time when division has dismayed me,
I have seen the gulf widen between men,
heard the bitter stream of words that
became a moat isolating one man from another,
seen the violence with which frightened men,
feeling threatened, have abused and crushed
those they believed to be enemies;

the time when illness has come,
and my body that until then had been familiar
 became unpredictable,
the senses that had given me pleasure were
 filled with pain,
and I was afraid;

the time when I feared for a loved one,
felt isolated from them in their pain,
knowing that I could offer only sympathy
 and try to understand what they were bearing—
sometimes I prayed that I might share the pain,
take something out of their body into mine
 —we can share so much else
  why not the pain, Lord?

These were the times when I asked for healing, Lord,
 and You heard me.

There has been a balm poured into the wound,
 a love that has bound up the broken flesh,
 a kindness that has nursed us back to strength:
we didn't always see it at the time or know
 what was happening to us,
but it was there,
a love that turned pain, adversity and hurt
 to our good,
  teaching us a truth we would never have learned
  otherwise,
  like bringing a resurrection out of a crucifixion.

Lord, in the time of our need,
 may we know that You are not hostile,

standing against us with the powers of hell:
may there be within us a certainty that pain cannot shake,
    a quiet faith that all things are for our healing—
    we shall not be broken.

IV

A Time to Weep —
and a Time to Laugh

IN THE DEPTHS

Out of the depths I cry to thee, O Lord! Psalm 130: 1

LORD, WE SOMETIMES make our bed in hell,
>if hell it has to be then best make it as comfortable
>>as possible,
>a bed is for rest and sleeping
>and maybe eyelids can close and consciousness drift
>>out of the hostile darkness.

Maybe 'hell' is too strong a word,
>but things are always relative.
>We might find 'hobgoblins and foul fiends' reassuring
>compared to the faceless anxiety that threatens us
>and the fear that rises out of our unconscious mind,
>its roots hidden from our view,
>a squalid weed with tendrils that go down
>>into darkness.

I do not invite the devil who comes
>to sit astride my bending mind,
>who twists the words of friends,
>makes furtive hate out of innocent circumstance,
>undermines achievements and applauds failures,

isolates me that I might be his kingdom
unassailed by faith, or hope,
or charity:
he is my enemy
and yet he is me,
if he were outside, other than I am,
then war could be declared,
white knight against black knight,
    stalking each other in grotesque
    movements—
but he is inside,
the solid yet unseen mercury that makes
    a mirror in my soul,
to be scraped away before the mirror becomes
    a window,
through which to see darkly into heaven.

Miserere, Domine.

Lord, there is more of You than I understand,
    even as there is more of myself than I know:
        may part of You that I do not see
        be present in the depths
            where anxieties flourish
            and stealthy darkness invades my
                waking hours,
            where the roots grip
            and the principalities and powers struggle
                over my destiny.

Be there, Lord,
    that I may not settle for the compromise
    of a bed in hell;
    be there,

so that as I see the black earth stir,
and an arm stretch through the mouldering leaves
    of autumn,
a hand reach out of corrupting darkness
to catch the setting sun,
I may not fear Him who rises from
    my corruption;
may I steadfastly look for His face
    and see the devil I fear
    is the Christ I love.

2

IN THE HEIGHTS

And Peter said to Jesus, "Lord, it is well that we are here . . ."
Matthew 17: 4

LORD, WE DO not always trust ecstasy,
    we dare not,
    the higher the pinnacle on which we stand
    the clearer we see the depths to which we can fall,
    the more sweet our joy
    the more bitter our sadness:
        ecstasy and depression, a hair's breadth divides
        them,
        the light of one creates the darkness of the
        other.

We even distrust it in the church, Lord;
    ecstasy is men speaking with tongues,
    experience out-stripping language,
    reality leaving understanding breathless and lost,
        but we want to verbalise, to explain,
            to take the divine encounter quickly
            out of the fire
            and cool it with apathy
            and wrap it in words;

74

ecstasy is the Ghostly flame quivering above
our heads,
igniting passion,
scorching the tongue with altar coals,
>   but hot heads are not for reasonable men,
>   passion is for lovers and not
>   the circumspect,
>   and better a silent tongue than a
>   scorched one:

ecstasy is grace and gratitude,
it is the apocalyptic thunder of the redeemed
recalling, in blood-washed purity, the tribulation
out of which they were brought,
>   but our gratitude lacks their intensity,
>   we will not see how dark is the
>   darkness,
>   we settle for the sins we can confess
>   and hide from those we can't.

Yet, Lord, in spite of fear and caution,
You give us ecstasy,

the moments that are lived and not explained
when joy leaves us speechless,
and our hands speak for us,
and the body of our flesh trembles
with the rapture of our spirit;
the moments when the Spirit breaks into
our plans, comes unannounced on our agendas,
and we who speak of crucifixion and resurrection
no longer speak
but feel holy pain and stir in life eternal;

the moments when grace forgives us,
we breathe freely
as the sin we know meets the mercy we know
and Christ hurls our guilt into the
    timeless and forgetting sea.

Lord, help us to stand at the summit
    where heaven meets earth in the moment of ecstasy,
        and if afterwards joy leaves us
        may that which gave it birth remain.

3

IN BETWEEN

In quietness and in trust shall be your strength. Isaiah 30: 15

LORD, MOST DAYS are ordinary days,
    filled with ordinary things,
        we work,
        we move among familiar people,
            nothing happens to make our life any different
                from what it was yesterday
            nor to make us expect any change for tomorrow.
In moments of ecstasy we resent ordinary things,
    they are an intrusion,
    they grip us by the ankles and drag us down to earth,
    we want to build tabernacles, not listen to the cry for
help.
In moments of depression we fear ordinary things,
    the tasks that suddenly seem too much for us,
    the people we fear will expect more than we
            have to give,
    the racking wheel going daily round,
        allowing no escape.

Yet, Lord, our ecstasy is formed of ordinary things,
    and our depression has to face our enemies
        on familiar ground,

it is the part in between,
    lower than ecstasy
    higher than depression,
    that gives our lives their meanings:
    we see You transfigured on the heights
        and we stammer for the glory,
    we cry for You in our depths
        and Calvary is beneath us,
    but every day, in ordinary things,
    You are revealing Yourself to us,
        You are as recognisable as broken bread,
        in the pattern of our lives
            Your word is heard as grace and truth.

Lord, we see You in reason,
    though sometimes we despise it,
    it is too cautious, we say,
    we clap a hand on our heart—this is what we
        think with, we say,
    reason is too cool,
    it is arrogant, we say,—we quote the folly of the
    cross as excuse for our stupidity and obtuseness;
    but, Lord, it is Your gift
        and when we have heard the chanting slogans,
        the screaming banners,
        when our sensibilities have reeled
        punch-drunk from shouts, half-formed impressions
        and the blows of mass media's bully-boys
        —then we turn with gratitude to reason,
        unadorned and vulnerable,
        whose way is patient
        and strength without force of arms.

Lord, we see You in the daily shape of our lives,
the friends who tread the way with us,
whose eccentricities we know and, better,
who have already accepted us with our faults,
the daily work, undramatic yet offering pride
in the skills we use and the experience we have
gained;
and the daily signs:
the worn pages of a Bible, a pen, a wedding ring,
a cross-word puzzle, elevenses, piano keys,
a photograph, a city street, a tree,
clouds, a light switch, voices
    —any could become ecstasy,
        all rescue us from despair.

4

THE LAUGH-MAKERS

Then our mouth was filled with laughter . . . Psalm 126: 2

LORD, THANK YOU for funny people:

thank You for the ones who don't mean to be funny,
the solemn and the uncertain who take themselves seriousl
and expect everyone else to do the same—
men in peaked caps,
wobbly contraltos,
family planning crusaders,
'experts' dragged into the television studio—so willingly-
    to speak the latest irrelevant word on
    the latest relevant crisis,
life-guards on Bognor Regis beach,
beauty queens;

thank You for the ones who have a sense of humour,
the friends who take the steam out of a situation
    by making us laugh,
the companions who share our private jokes,
people who see the funny side of anything—
you know, banana-peel humour,

the witty and the sharp who make conversation a pleasure,
the cheerful who refuse to be knocked down;

thank You for the eccentric,
that man with the model railway lay-out,
sold us tickets when we went in to see it,
then put on a railway hat, blew a whistle,
    waved a flag,
and pushed the switch to send the 9.15 out of
    King's Cross,
and not a smile on his face,
just a gleam of ecstasy in his eyes;

thank You for the clowns,
the brave men who stand at the intersections of life
where tears and laughter cross
and comedy confronts tragedy,
who take the tensions of our human life
and redeem the darkness with laughter;

thank You for comedians,
the Keystone cops and the Marx brothers,
Hancock, and Chaplin,
Andy Williams' bear, doomed to go without his
    milk and cookies.

ord, thank You for funny people,
    may they show us ourselves:
    when we are pompous and silly asses,
    when we refuse to see the humour in any situation,
    when we fail to see our own eccentricities
    and are too proud to be clowns.

Lord, there are so many fine things we would like to do,
    loving, serving, leading, inspiring—
    all noble aims:
    but teach us that there is another vocation,
    to make people laugh.

5

LAUGHTER IN PARADISE

Rejoice in the Lord always; again I will say, Rejoice. Philippians 4: 4

LORD, IT IS SAID there is laughter in Paradise,
   which isn't quite what we expected.

You can see we don't expect it by the way we worship You,
here and now;
   a lecturer on preaching once told us (solemnly),
   "Gentlemen, the pulpit is not the place for laughter"—
   heaven help the pulpit!

It's so different with all those Latin races,
   they turn religion into a festival,
   a carnival of flowers and dancing,
   a public holiday with processions, bright-coloured saints,
   incense-swinging priests, and hand-clapping children,
   all of which makes our Protestant short back-and-sides
         stand on end.

Lord, we have learned to praise You in brown Bethels,
   strong in their simplicity but hard on the eye.
   And we've encouraged so many odd traditions—

Sunday 'best', soggy organs, straw hats,
and pious smiles—so much less vulgar than
a belly laugh.

Things are changing slightly,
    there are the boys with their long hair like cheerful Elijahs
    and flower shirts and velvet trousers,
    and girls in dancing minis and gliding maxis,
    there are more shiny boots than straw hats,
    people don't look quite so up-tight.

But we still find it hard to see worship as a celebration, Lord
    we feel we must be serious with that bread and wine
        on the Table,
    symbols of broken body and poured out blood,
    reminders of suffering and death,
    spurs to penitence and renewal
        —but that's only the half
        if this is truly a sacrament.

Lord, this Table is spread with our daily bread,
    and wine that makes men merry,
    they are what they are as well as that which they
        symbolise—
    they are a feast,
    we raise our glasses in a toast to the God of the
        new Covenant,
    we drink our own health and God's glory.

Lord, may there be laughter in Bethel as well as in Paradise,
    may we celebrate, here and now,

because You are with us,
You are here, amongst us
—the bridegroom has come,
Lord, tell us the one about the plank and the splinter.

V

A Time to Mourn — and a Time to Dance

THE LAST ENEMY

Jesus said to her, "Woman, why are you weeping . . . ?" John 20: 15

LORD, THE JOYOUS confidence of Easter Sunday can be a long
    way from the grief of bereavement and the fear of death:
    we have Your promise that those who mourn shall be
       comforted,
    those who weep shall laugh,
    but mourning does not end, it only numbs with age,
    and it seems that comfort doesn't reach the depth of
       the wound,
    and weeping ends long before laughter comes.

There were some for whom death was the last benediction,
    people who, like Simeon, embraced the Word of life
    and were content to depart, having seen Your salvation:
        like Annie, in her nineties (she was thirty when
        Queen Victoria died!), nimble mind,
        saucy humour, earthy faith,
        who fell asleep in Christ.
    But there were the others, Lord:
        the young ones, the strong ones,
        for some there was no warning, no preparation,

death came as unexpected as a shaft of lightning
    out of a cloudless sky,
and those who loved them had to bear shock
    as well as grief,
for one day life had been full and the next it
    was empty,
they looked stunned and grey for months afterward

And there were the ones who could not die,
    though their bodies were tired and their eyes
    set on the city to come, yet death was
    loath to meet them and life had abandoned
    them to weariness,
    it is the way of things, for some death comes
    too soon,
    and for some it is too late.

And there were the ones for whom death was a release from
    pain's pitiless captivity;
    I remember the last time I visited Kathleen,
    they had moved her bed in the ward,
    and unawares I walked straight past her,
    I couldn't find her,
    I had to ask the nurse which one she was,
    a few days, that's all, and her sunken face
    no longer recognisable.

Lord, may Easter Sunday speak to us in our pain,
    and shock, and bereavement, and dying:
    You have taken this mortal flesh,
    You trod the lingering road down into death,
    You have accepted the corruption and decay of the bod
        You are risen because You died.

Help us, Lord,
    when we grieve,
    when we are afraid,
    when the days are slow to heal,
        help us, Lord,
            You have been here before us.

2

RESURRECTION

"Lord, when did we see thee hungry or thirsty or a stranger or nake
or sick or in prison, and did not minister to thee?" Matthew 25: 44

LORD, IT'S NEARLY two thousand years since they found
        the empty tomb,
        the folded grave-clothes,
        the broken seals,
        the great stone rolled away:
  two thousand years since the message ran from
  mouth to mouth, "Christ is Risen!"
        and soldiers quaked,
        and priests quivered,
        and Mary wept,
        and disciples waited,
        and Thomas doubted.

And that's what we celebrate, Lord—Easter Sunday,
     the great day,
     beautiful hymns,
     spring flowers, yellow, gold and white,
     lilies, bowed in chastity;
     it's a beautiful time, Lord,

so beautiful that we no longer quake, quiver,
 weep, wait and doubt when we are
 told that Christ is risen.

It is spring-time, we say, and Jesus risen is like
 the flowers breaking out of winter's earth,
 the daffodil becomes the symbol of resurrection,
 the long night of winter is ended,
 the trees begin to hide their gaunt limbs
  beneath the green livery of leaf and blossom;
 spring is resurrection and resurrection is spring.
Lord, we are drunk with the beauty of it,
 and sometimes the beauty hides the terror,
 the pity, the joy and the uncertainty,
 like plastic grass around an open grave
 concealing the raw earth in which our mortal
 bodies are laid.

What is the resurrection, Lord?
 It is Lazarus, rising from the grave,
 bound in shrouds, stinking with
 the corruption that is death;
 it is Paul, harried and tormented
 all the way to Damascus, pursued
 by a Christ Who will not die;
 it is Peter, unstable Rock made strong,
 crucified head down in the fellowship
 of Christ's sufferings, Who is risen
 from the dead;
 it is the stare of the hungry that
 rivets my pity,
 the squalor of the homeless,
 too near for comfort,

the cry that asks for peace,
the hands that reach for bread
in the world where the face of Jesus
cannot be erased from the face of the poor;
it is Christ, here and now,
disturbing our apathetic sleep,
pursuing us with truth that gives our lies no rest,
stabbing pity awake,
burning our lips with the word of eternal life.

Lord, the flowers are beautiful,
but they are not enough to make us
quake, quiver, weep, wait and doubt.

3

THE PARADISE POLKA

*e went out, and saw a tax collector, named Levi, and he said to him,
"Follow Me." Luke 5: 27*

ORD, YOU LEAD us in the dance of life,
    for dance it is, this pilgrimage of ours,
    the dance of summer days
    and the leap amongst the thunder clouds,
    a pirouette in the teeming rain
    and the slow shuffle of the mourner.

ou call us to joy, Lord,
    and always it is joy,
    like the joy of a clown who makes laughter
        out of comedy and tragedy,
            hope and despair,
            the past and the future:
clowns—
I once saw a picture of Christ crucified as a clown,
it seemed like blasphemy at first,
but it wasn't—
clowns stand at the inter-sections of life
where tears and laughter cross,
they ignore neither,

and that's what our following and our believing are
about—God works together with all things.

Lord, I sometimes lose faith in the dance,
    feet heavy with sadness or disappointment
    I complain that life is a funeral march after all:
    but then there's the music, always the music,
        "Be of good cheer!"
        Brahms,
        a telephone call,
        a letter,
        thanks for what I did when I thought
            I had done nothing,
        a jet over-head, flying West (memories),
        a laugh—
    these are the sounds of music, making my
        dragging feet tap into life again,
    calling me to follow the dancing Jesus.

Lord, life is good,
    all of it!
    That's not to say it's easy,
        or without pain,
        to say that would make me half a clown,
        a counterfeit, trifling with laughs and
            ignoring the tears.
    Yet when it has been difficult,
        when there has been pain,
        when things have gone bad,
        still at the end of it, I've wanted to stay alive,
        —is it wrong, Lord,
            sometimes being drunk with the pleasure of
            living?

'm following, Lord,
    I'm watching Your feet when the steps are difficult,
    but we're dancing, Lord,
    the paradise polka.

4

A DANCING HIPPIE

Consider the lilies of the field, how they grow; they neither toil nor spin
yet I tell you, even Solomon in all his glory was not arrayed like one of
these. Matthew 6: 28

LORD, WE ARE bringing beauty back to the world,
    for beauty has been sleeping, guarded by
        the Beast:
    beauty flows, like a satin shirt in a breeze,
        or trailing chiffon, dancing like Isadora
        in a purple noon,
        or hair, caught in a wind,
        black hair, framing dark eyes,
            tumbling over shoulders to waist,
        brown hair, swirling in ringlets,
        fair hair, washed in the sun,
        hair, hair, that grows like freedom;
        beauty is in beads that sway,
        a rainbow around our necks,
        cheap beads, all colours except the red of blood
            with which men buy diamonds;
        beauty is in flowers,
        petals running through hair,
            sweet as purity and lovely as peace.

ord, we are bringing love back to the world,
    for love has had a boot upon her neck,
    and a rifle at her back:
    love flows, as hand touches hand,
        and looking eyes speak, he and she,
        moments no longer in time;
        love is in hands that pluck strings,
        strumming out peace, justice and brotherhood,
            songs for battles without weapons
            and warfare without blood,
        freedom for you and freedom for me,
        your place is my place
            and my place is your place,
        we share the earth,
        take down the doors,
        abandon the detached and the semi-detached,
        we sit in a circle that is widening
            like a ripple,
        bringing everybody in to be loved.

ord, we ask for beauty and love,
    this is our thing,
    this scene has all the ugliness it needs
        and there was never enough love.
We ask what He asked,
        Who saw more beauty in a Galilean
        flower than in the chipped diamonds,
        golden rods, silver dishes, marble pillars,
        clanking armoury of a king's palace;
        Who offered love to everyone,
        even the unwanted, and the hated, and the feared,
        to the old and the young,
        and the good and the bad.

99

Lord, that was what He asked for,
    beauty and love,
        and where else shall we find them,
           but in Him?

5

THE DISCOTHEQUE

Again you shall adorn yourself with timbrels, and shall go forth in the dance of the merrymakers. Jeremiah 31: 4

LORD, IT HAS to be dark,
    electric lights are for railway stations and bank offices,
    it helps us to see each other, which is all right,
    but it shows the distance between us as well;
    light shows up the room,
    we can admire the wallpaper, rave about the
        Scandinavian furniture, envy the velvet drapes,
    but that distracts from the people,
    we are looking at things not at one another;
it has to be dark,
    in the dark there is no distance,
    the wallpaper doesn't matter, walls are the
        four limits of our darkness,
    here it is only people that have meaning,
    people who move, sway, touch, snap fingers,
        play with beads, clutch Coke straws.

And the darkness brings the music nearer,
    the amplifier rocks to the pounding beat,
    the room holds its sides for the high notes,
    people try to talk to each other over the endless sound,

they carefully mouth their words,
then laugh, and shrug their shoulders,
the music wins:
the dancers move around, vaguely in pairs,
never touching, stalking each other and hitting
the air like happy-go-lucky boxers who have
forgotten the fight:
the mood changes,
they go girlishly gay with Mary Hopkin,
dream with Simon and Garfunkel,
sway, shut-eyed and sullen, with the Stones,
fall in love with Cliff and Herman,
go mystic with the Beatles.

Even in the dark, there is colour, Lord,
a blonde tosses her hair,
rows of beads sway with the rhythm,
crosses, as big as an archbishop's, hang
waist-high,
coloured shoes flash,
boys' shirts, pink, green, scarlet, blue,
covered with flowers shaken out
of a shaggy head,
girls shimmer, drenched in "Wet Look".

This room, this music, these people,
it's all for real,
the scene they made themselves,
doing their own thing,
trying to find themselves away from a world
that adds up the 'O' levels,
believes in 'short back and sides',
and rarely shows enthusiasm.

Lord, for some of them You are as real as that room,
    You are set firmly in their scene,
    faith hasn't destroyed their gaiety:
        which is amazing really, Lord,
        seeing they are usually expected
        to find You amongst the pitch-pine pews
        to the accompaniment of Isaac Watts.

VI

A Time to Keep —
and a Time to Cast Away

1

IN A CINEMA

He changes times and seasons . . . Daniel 2: 21

LORD, THEY USED to call them picture palaces,
    and that's what they were,
    with entrance halls of glass and chrome,
    deep plush carpets that hushed our feet into awe,
    crystal chandeliers and sweeping stairways;
    inside, eyes accustomed to the dark,
    you could see pillars on the wall and carvings
        like a Gothic temple,
    and hundreds of seats facing the great screen
        —the screen,
    where the deities of Hollywood descended
    to the plains of mortal men,
    where our hopes were lived out for us
    and our battles won,
    where we were carried away to worlds
    of fantasy that became more real than
    the grey world that greeted our blinking eyes
    when the show was over.

We used to glow with anticipation
    when we went to the pictures, Lord,

stand an hour in the queue for the one-and-threes,
hold our breath as the commissionaire came to count
    out the first twenty,
grin with satisfaction when we were among them,
get inside and into our seats as quickly as possible;
there was no moment like the drawing of the flashy
    curtains,
    then the credits,
    preceded by that lion roaring, fit to devour us,
    or the rippling-muscled man ceaselessly
        banging his gong:
    then we were away, and reality slipped
        rapidly in our wake.

It's different now—
    they only show films four nights a week;
    the other three its big Bingo,
    the new paradise, the new escape,
    we don't dream our way out now, we try to buy it.
And there's more people for Bingo than for the films;
now the entrance halls are like old railway stations,
inside the twenty people in the audience have a
    hundred seats each,
the film goes on as if nobody were watching it,
people are too embarrassed to laugh in the
    lonely darkness,
and the old-age pensioners are more grateful
    for the warmth than for the film.

It's different now, Lord,
    the crowds have gone,
    the cinemas stand like massive memorials to
    an age that died only yesterday.

ord, the Church is a bit like that,
    buildings left from the days when chapels were palaces
        and the pulpit a throne,
    remnants of a different age and way of life,
    tempted sometimes to offer gimmicks instead of
        the word of life:
    You don't change, Lord,
    You are always in front of us,
    when we remember how things used to be
        may we hope for what they shall be.

2

IN A STREET MARKET

For here we have no lasting city, but we seek the city which is to come
Hebrews 13: 14

LORD, THEY COME here early,
    pushing cumbersome carts loaded with the day's wares,
    the regular ones, making straight for their "pitch",
    the casual ones, hoping to set up shop in a free space:
    in minutes the deserted street seems to have
        spawned a community,
    the grey, rain-washed pavements are hidden
        by moving feet,
    the gutter has taken on the dignity of the sales counter.

It's all here,
    vegetable stalls, potatoes big as fists,
    plain green cabbages, tomatoes with reminders of sunshine
    stiff-backed celeries, mushrooms morning-gathered,
    tousle-topped carrots, tear-bringing onions;
    there's the stall with curtain materials,
    billowing nets, flowers a shade too vulgar,
    cubes and circles ("very contempory, ducky"),
    soft velvet;

there's the cosmetics stall,
bottles of hair-cream big enough to keep
    a regiment of heads in place,
tooth-paste, with man's newest answer to decay,
cheap soap, eye-watering perfume;
and there's the bargain stall,
where the best buy in town is to be found,
the stall-holder isn't asking one-fifty,
nor one twenty-five, not even a pound,
seventy-five pence would be a give-away,
fifty, who'll have one for fifty?
only fifty pence!
the gaping crowd driven down the spiral of
    price descent
fumbles nervously for its coins to claim the
    prize before it vanishes.

There are all sorts of people here, Lord,
    pensioners clutching their purses—how many potatoes
        do you buy when you live on your own?
    husbands, bored to tears, loaded with the
        week's shopping—no equality of the sexes here!
    a group of giggling girls,
    Rosie, hair piled precariously high, glamour girl
        of the market, fifty if she's a day:
and the odd snippets of conversation heard in the passing
("She said we'd 'ave to buy 'er a maxi-coat.
But I said to 'er, I said, 'You're only
firteen—wha' d'you want wiv a maxi-coat?'
I said")
    shuffling, jostling, smiling, staring,
    they come and go all day, people always on
    the move.

You said the Church should be like that, Lord,
    not a permanent fixture, but on the move,
    carrying its wealth around,
    offering its good news where people need it
        and people can receive it,
    exposed to sun and storm,
    at risk, transitory, passing through.
But we prefer the prestige, the solid building,
    we want a continuing city,
    not for us the exposure of the market,
    for us the security of those who are
    on the inside, looking out.

3

AT THE PROMS

David also commanded the chiefs of the Levites to appoint their brethren as the singers who should play loudly on musical instruments, on harps and lyres and cymbals, to raise sounds of joy. 1 Chronicles 15: 16

LORD, IT'S NEVER quite the same up here in the stalls,
    it's almost like cheating,
    sitting whilst the others stand,
    or a sign that one has grown older,
    and moved up from the arena where the life is
    to the stalls where we are spectators.

Memories crowd in—they shouldn't yet, memories can
    make the past more precious than the present
    —they shouldn't, but they do,
    and perhaps we can be forgiven because
    everything looks as it always did:
        this great hall, another memorial
        to dear Albert;
        the bust of Henry Wood
        looking down on us;
        the fountain and fish-pond in the middle,
        so cool on a summer's evening;
        and the promenaders,

hair a curl longer,
clothes a riot,
but as much captives of enchantment
as were we.

Remember the *Evening News* spread out on the floor
on which we sat, back to back?
that solemn, spotty-faced boy who exhorted
me to persevere with Bartok—sure to make
sense one day?
that 'cellist, forget his name, who pulled
such peculiar faces whilst he was playing
that they got the giggles in the front row?
a night never forgotten, an engagement ring,
the third Brandenburg, Knightsbridge on a summer's
evening?
Malcolm Sargent, baton uplifted,
a flourish, and the music soaring into the spaces?
the last night,
when we sang *Land of Hope and Glory*
and knew that our land had long been
deprived of that sort of hope and
stripped of that sort of glory,
yet the music encouraging us to believe
that there might be a hope and a glory
that could be ours,
without war and bloodshed,
without conquest,
without the pride of race and blood?

It still looks the same, Lord,
and music still works its miracle,
as we listen with our memories and with our hopes,

as we sit, men at the feast,
tasting, at this latest hour of mankind,
the creative wealth of the centuries.

Lord, I remember my dreams as I listened,
down there in the arena where they stand now,
and some of my dreams came true
and some shall yet come true—
may it be so for them;
Lord, You were there then,
You are here now,
and that's what has filled the years with gratitude—
may it be so for them.

4

NEW YEAR'S EVE

Lord, Thou hast been our dwelling place in all generations.
Psalm 90: 1

LORD, TODAY I remember another year of my life,
and another year of my dying,
another twelve months in the journey
from my birth to my death,
this day reminds me that time passes,
and all my time is part of Your eternity:
Lord, who gave me life in my mother's
womb,
who shall give me life again in
death's consummation.

Thank You, Lord, for this year:
thank You for the work that has filled my days,
sometimes it has been rewarding, intense with meaning,
it has borne fruit in others and in myself,
sometimes it has been frustrating, a task to be done,
not because the spirit was urgent and the will responsive
but simply because it was there—
but Lord, how much worse if the task had not been there
and my hands compelled to hang idle

and my mind denied the discipline of change,
circumstance and problem;
thank You for the people who have filled my days,
those nearest who have continued to find something
in me to love and have called love out of me,
those who have shared with me in the worship
and witness of the Church,
those who trusted me in their own time of need,
and those who walked with me in mine,
and people, just people,
bowler-hatted, overalled, brief-cased,
baggy-trousered, mini-skirted, maxi-coated,
laughing, scowling, blue-eyed, red-haired,
busy, eccentric people;
thank You, Lord, for beauty,
the Epping trees at spring-time,
the Manhattan sky-line,
a forgotten Brahms melody heard again,
the Mozart twenty-first piano concerto,
Picasso's "Tragedy",
the faith and gaiety of "Fiddler on the Roof",
and books,
enlightening, puzzling, moving, infuriating;

Lord, this is my year, thank You.

Today I am wealthy.
Lord, I pray for others who are poor in ways
that I have been poor and may yet be poor:
be with those for whom the chill wind
of loneliness comes sighing out of tomorrow,
those whose bodies are weakened by
pain, disease and age who remember
the strength of former years,

those who feel that the pattern of their lives
is set, yet yearn for change,
those who know that life's richest gifts
have already been given.

Lord, may gratitude mingle with hope
for all of us,
You are our past, our present and our future,
the Alpha of our birth,
the Omega of our death,
You have brought our lives
from time into eternity.

VII

A Time for War —
and a Time for Peace

THE DESTRUCTION THAT WASTES AT NOONDAY

And you will hear of wars and rumours of wars . . . Matthew 24: 6

LORD, FROM San Francisco to Vladivostok,
    men are going about their daily business:
        they bury old institutions, and conceive
        new ones in their dreams,
        they fall in love, marry, and beget
        children,
        they work today, and make plans for
        tomorrow,
        they invest their money, trusting that
        time will give the increase,
            —men living as if the future were
        never in doubt,
        yet knowing the sinister threat,
        the ultimate horror upon which their
        security rests.

For we know, Lord, that one day
    the monster could rise like Leviathan from the
    depths of the sea
    and in the pillar of smoke, the mushroom
    spawning decay,

announce Armageddon, the sentence of
death making us
    the last generation of man.

We know, Lord, that our peace rests upon the
    threat of our extinction,
    the dark shadow of a future day in
    which
        the earth would turn to dust
        and the sun stop still in the
            mid-day sky,
        our blood would bubble, and our
            flesh turn to lava,
        a day in which the only mercy would
            be the mercy of death.

From San Francisco to Vladivostok they know
    it must be peace or extermination—please Lord,
    they do know, don't they?
    but in Israel and Egypt, in Africa,
    in Vietnam, war continues,
    fought with conventional weapons,
    contained within reasonable limits:
        they rip men's stomachs with "conventional"
            bayonets,
        they split their bones and riddle their muscles
            with "conventional" bullets,
        they tear men's flesh and spill men's blood
            with "conventional" bombs,
        they sear men's bodies
            with "conventional" flame-throwers,
        and burst men's lungs
            with "conventional" gas;

they contain war within the "reasonable" limits
  of two hundred Biafran children dying
  from hunger within a week,
  a regiment of Arabs, dead and rotting
  in the desert sun,
  six hundred Vietcong wiped out in a single raid,
  and two hundred and fifty American soldiers
  killed in one week.

Lord, defend us from the blasphemy of our language,
  lest speaking of "conventional weapons"
  and "reasonable" limits,
  we forget the horror that is war;
    the wars we know
    are no more tolerable than
      the Armageddon we do not.

REMEMBRANCE SUNDAY

It is the Lord our God who brought us and our fathers up from the land of Egypt, out of the house of bondage . . . Joshua 24: 17a

LORD, WE HAVE grown to hate war,
    for war can make an end of us,
    destroying in a moment the race of men
    You brought to birth through patient
    millenniums,
    leaving our planet to hurl about the sun,
    dead and dusty like the moon.

Lord, our hatred for war
    sometimes turns in contempt to the wars that
    have been,
    and cynicism sours the remembrance of the men
    who fought them
        —it is a human failing, Lord,
        we always know better than our fathers,
        forgetting that we know what our fathers
            taught us,
            the lessons they learned in the fury
            of battle.

Lord, today we would remember them,
    not in cynicism but in sorrow;
    we remember men who, though outnumbered,
        resisted an invader,
    believing it right to defend this island,
        their families and their friends,
    against the onslaught of an enemy
        who turned a daydream into a nightmare,
    drunk with the ancient poisons
        of race and blood;

    we remember brave men,
    who first defeated their own fear,
    climbing into the perilous sky
        to pit skill and fragile metal
        against a black Armada,
    a pitiful few against the pitiless many;

    we remember men who kept their humanity
        in the savagery of battle,
    men who in days of peace had delivered milk,
        sold bread, grown roses,
        stood at cash desks, cut cloth,
        caught the 8.15 to town,
    and in war willed to die that others might live,
    displaying the courage of those who do not choose
        to be heroes;

    we remember civilians of occupied countries who
        lived through the humiliation of defeat,
    heard the sound of jackboots in their streets
        and alien voices at their doors,
    yet refused the demeanour of slavery,

and waited for freedom with the same certainty
    that men wait for the sun to rise
    on another day;

we remember those who lived through
    the inhumanity of the concentration camps,
robbed of their identity,
subject to the whims of the lawless
    and the threat of the gas-chamber,
who yet remained human,
    comforted one another
    and even forgave their tormentors.

Lord, as we turn in horror from war
    may we not turn away from those
        who, before our birth, fought our battles.

        We can renounce war, because we are free;
        we are free, because our fathers
            fought and died.

3

WINNING THE PEACE

*He shall judge between the nations, and shall decide for many peoples;
and they shall beat their swords into plowshares and their spears into
pruning hooks . . . Isaiah 2: 4*

LORD, IN TIME of war we solve our problems:
>   we find a unity that had hitherto eluded us,
>   men divided by class, upbringing and status
>   find common cause and face the enemy
>   as comrades in arms,
>   they discover the humanity they share
>   in the instinct for survival;
>   new techniques are invented,
>   technology becomes a willing servant,
>   we discover in war the skills
>   that had escaped us in peace:
>   supplies are maintained,
>   men are fed and clothed,
>   food is shared,
>   hunger and poverty are bad for morale
>   so we ensure that every man's need is met.

Lord, that's how it is in war,
>   in peace there is no urgency,
>   and our problems settle upon us like dust;

each man fights his own enemy,
the enemy that threatens his rights
and assails his self-interest,
we are divided again by class and privilege,
the brotherhood of battle is forgotten
as our personal desires outweigh
the common good;

the skills learned quickly in war
come slowly in peace,
there's never enough money,
school buildings decay
and we have flag days for medical research:

and charity was never so compelling
as necessity, morale no longer matters,
so the poor may grow poorer,
and the cause of justice sounds no trumpet
to unrelenting warfare.

Lord, summon us to peace,
grant us discipline,
may love direct our anger,
and may we fight to the death the
enemies of man's spirit.

Help us, Lord, to storm the barriers
that divide men, the lies, the propaganda,
the inflammatory words, the half-truths
that separate us;

help us, Lord, to organise our public
life for the common weal,

to wrestle against inefficiency,
stupidity, obsolescence, bureaucracy,
and the petty-mindedness that jealously guards
the *status quo*
and resists the coming of the
future;

help us, Lord, to fight injustice as
an alien intruder upon our territory,
to conquer poverty and defeat hunger,
to resist every foe that degrades
the life of man.

Lord, we have yet to win our peace,
may the treason of indifference not keep us
from the noise of battle.

4

A GODLY REVOLUTION

He has shown strength with his arm, he has scattered the proud in the imagination of their hearts, he has put down the mighty from their thrones, and exalted those of low degree; he has filled the hungry with good things, and the rich he has sent empty away. Luke 1: 51–53

LORD, IT'S TIME for a change,
    that's why we are marching,
        marching to change the world:
    we are tired of sleepy, middle-aged people
    who believe in nothing,
    have given up God for Bingo,
    will vote for the party that will feather their nest,
    because that's all they want, a nest,
    cosy, sound-proof, comfortable,
    with television as the only window,
    ten pennies a year conscience money to Oxfam,
    and the second car
    purring contentedly outside;
    we are tired of a society that allows injustice,
    which violates some people because they weren't born here
    or their skin is black,
    which violates others
    by forcing them to live in squalor and poverty,

which spends millions on arms
and allows schools to rot
and the poor to grow poorer;
we are tired of a world that settles
its arguments with brute force,
burning, shelling, bombing,
fighting wars in which flesh is ripped from bone,
the stench of burning flesh fills the nostrils,
metal is driven into men's bodies,
women weep and children tremble, soldiers die,
and nobody wins for there is no meaning
to victory;
we are tired of being told what we
ought to do by people who don't
know what *they* ought to do,
being lectured about morality by people without morals,
being counselled about love by people who are loveless,
being exhorted to think of others by people
who are selfish.

Lord, we are marching,
    the banners are flying,
        friends at right and left, the rumbling
        sound of feet,
            slogans flung like bombs into the
            barricades of those who want nothing
            to be changed.

Lord, our cause is just,
    but I have fears:
        I fear that when our youth is passed
        our dreams shall die, and we too will
        settle for indifference;

I fear that when we meet those whose
cause we fight, that we shall be repelled,
that our love shall be for a cause and
not for people;
I fear that we shall become violent
like the violence we fight, that we shall
find blood on our own hands;
I fear that we will no longer believe
there is right and wrong, good and evil:
>   Lord, these are my fears
>   that rise up when the march
>   is over,
>   and the shouts have died,
>   and I am alone.

Lord, I take the cross as my sign,
>   for You changed the world,
>   You showed us the power of truth
>   and love and goodness,
>   at Calvary You received the anger and
>   the violence of others,
>   bore it in Your own body,
>   and in that terrible moment of
>   cruelty and suffering opened
>   our eyes to the strong love of God:

>   Lord, in every cause for which I
>   fight,
>   may anger be held by love,
>   and Your truth
>   be my only passion.

5

THE DAY OF THE LORD

Then comes the end, when he delivers the kingdom to God the Father
after destroying every rule and every authority and power.
1 Corinthians 15: 24

LORD, WE ARE waiting for the Last Day,
    when from the four corners of earth the trumpets'
    fanfare will sound, and the sun will dim
    before the glory of Him Who comes as Son of Man,
    and down the avenues of the skies will come
    angels and archangels, and from the heights
    and out of the depths will be heard the
    new song, harmonies liberated in the praise
    of God:
    when glory will cover the face of the
    earth, burning out decay and corruption,
    purging it of impurity and mortality,
    turning the shimmering summer, the rusty autumn,
    the friendless winter, to the promise of spring;
    when the saints will come marching in,
    generation after generation of them,
    the martyrs, the prophets, the scholars,
    the mystics, the reformers, the warriors,
    Paul, Irenaeus, Augustine, Francis, Luther,

Helwys, Clifford, Forsyth, Bonhoeffer,
Teilhard
  and Annie, and Dick,
  Mary and young Virginia;
  when the Devil will be flung by
  his tail and hurled into the lake
  of brimstone and fire, which is the
  second death.

Lord, we are waiting for the Last Day,
  the end of the war,
  the day of our freedom, when destiny
    will strike the chain from our
    wrists,
  the day of our deliverance, when pain
    will be powerless,
  the day of our resurrection, when death
    cowers before the Lord
    of the third day,
  the day of our reconciliation, when
    all creation shall be gathered
    into Christ.

Lord, we are waiting for the Last Day,
  but there remains today,
    and our eyes peering to the horizon sometimes
      miss what is happening at our right hand
      and our left,
    there is a coming that still takes us unawares,
    a visitation humble and unannounced,
      like a baby born in poverty,
      a man riding upon a donkey,
      a gardener seen through tears.

Lord, You come to us,
  Your advent is here and now,
    give us eyes to see and faith to believe,
      lest the last trumpet sound on deaf ears,
      and our sleeping eyes do not see
        the glory:
      lest, living in hope,
        we know not faith or love.